BEST WALKS ON THE LOWER LAKELAND I
In the North-East

The head of Ullswater with Keldas and Birkhouse Moor in view

BEST WALKS ON THE LOWER LAKELAND FELLS

In the North-East

Bob Allen

MICHAEL JOSEPH
London

MICHAEL JOSEPH LTD

Published by the Penguin Group
27 Wrights Lane, London W8 5TZ
Viking Penguin Inc., 375 Hudson Street, New York, New York 10014, USA
Penguin Books Australia Ltd, Ringwood, Victoria, Australia
Penguin Books Canada Ltd, 10 Alcorn Avenue, Toronto, Ontario,
Canada M4V 3B2
Penguin Books (NZ) Ltd, 182–190 Wairau Road, Auckland 10, New Zealand

Penguin Books Ltd, Registered Offices: Harmondsworth, Middlesex, England

First published in Great Britain 1995

Typeset in 11/12pt Linotron Goudy Old Style by
Goodfellow and Egan Ltd. Cambridge
Made and printed in Singapore by
Kyodo Printing Co. (s) Pte Ltd.

ISBN 0 7181 3806 6

The moral right of the author has been asserted

Also by Bob Allen

ON HIGH LAKELAND FELLS
ON LOWER LAKELAND FELLS
ESCAPE TO THE DALES
ON FOOT IN SNOWDONIA
SHORT WALKS IN THE LAKE DISTRICT

CONTENTS

Acknowledgements

My debt to the Ordnance Survey and their wonderful maps will be self-evident. I have pored over them, searched my memories with their help and tramped over the fells with them in my pocket to remind me of details long forgotten.

My old friend Rob Rose accompanied me on several exploratory walks, my wife Lin and son Jonathan on others (and didn't complain much), but on the whole I have spent most of the time on the fells on my own with my two dogs, Henry and Freddie. Everybody else decided that waiting around while I took photographs was just too boring, so they left me to get on with it alone.

INTRODUCTION

This is an illustrated collection of ten of the best shorter fellwalks in the north-eastern part of the Lake District (including two which use a lake steamer on the approach). While I was completing my first Lakeland book, *On High Lakeland Fells*, I was aware that all the emphasis in that book was on the 'High' and that I was missing out some marvellous fells whose only difference was their comparative lack of height. So I started looking and surprised myself with the quality and quantity of excellent shorter walks that can be found. The average altitude of this collection is 1875ft/572m, average height gained is 1332ft/406m, average distance is 4½ miles/7.2 km, and the average time a little over three hours. All are 'rounds', enabling an easy return to the starting-point. If your own favourite fell is not included, that may be because I've tried to avoid overlapping with walks in the 'High Fells' book. If it's not in there, then I apologise: I had to draw a line somewhere.

The **Map:** All except one of the walks (Bowscale Fell) can be found on the Ordnance Survey Outdoor Leisure map, sheet 5, North Eastern area. However, don't rely too slavishly on the map: footpaths which are clearly marked on the map sometimes may be hardly distinguishable on the ground.

Distances: These are not exact, simply approximations based on the map.

'Highest elevation reached' and **'height gained':** These are the actual heights in feet above sea level (converted to metres) from precise figures on the map if given. If not, the height is my best assessment.

The **'star rating':** This is completely subjective. I have simply attempted to convey something of the overall quality of the walk. Fine mountain landscape and scenery and variety of interest are particularly important in this assessment. I know I have a definite preference for the wild places, the rough ground, the untracked rather than the smooth pathways and this will no doubt be sometimes apparent. I respond above all to fine landscape scenery. I go to the fells and mountains for exercise and recreation but I live for those moments when I just have to grab for my camera.

'General level of exertion required': The more steeply you go uphill the more likely you are to get puffed; a short but steep climb can be a lot more exhausting than a long level stroll. I have simply attempted to give some indication of what to expect.

'**Time for the round**': My times are not based on any formula, just an assessment based on my experience. They do *not* include lengthy lunch-stops.

'**Terrain**': In the introductory specifications for each walk I have added a few comments about the nature of the ground underfoot, which I hope will be helpful. Generally these refer to conditions in spring, summer or autumn; winter can introduce a new dimension of unpredictability which is the delight of experienced fellwalkers but could cause problems for beginners.

Clothing and footwear: The biggest cause of all accidents on the fells is slipping on wet grass and so the importance of suitable footwear – preferably warm, well-fitting, waterproof, giving support to the ankles and with suitably ridged soles – cannot be over-emphasised. Nor can I stress too strongly that mild, balmy weather in the valley can be transformed at 1500ft into something more like the Arctic; it helps enormously to wear clothing which minimises dampness caused by sweating and modern synthetic fabrics now do this. Mixing man-made and natural fibres defeats the object: wearing a Goretex-type breathable waterproof on top of a cotton shirt and a woollen jersey is unlikely to keep you dry.

Place names: I hope and believe I have used the spellings used on the OS map, but there are minor alterations from one edition of those maps to another, and from one scale to another, so it will depend which edition of the relevant map you are looking at. Also, the walking and climbing community use some names which you will not find on the OS map. Where relevant, I have mentioned these in the text but have used the OS names.

Grid references: It helps greatly in not getting lost if you start from the right place so I have provided a grid reference for the starting point of each walk. The National Grid Reference System is explained in the bottom right-hand corner of the Ordnance Survey map for anybody who isn't accustomed to using it. Correct use of a compass, including checking your bearing before you are overtaken by the mist, will minimise your mixing up your lefts with your rights and heading off down the wrong valley. By not heeding this advice myself in the Alps I once failed to climb the wrong route on the wrong mountain. Despite all your instincts to the contrary, the compass is almost never wrong: it is just you who are not where you thought you were.

Access: Across much of the Lake District there is a generally accepted freedom to roam on high land above the cultivated land or intake walls. It is essential, however, that public footpaths or permissive rights of way are used to reach the higher land and I have tried to ensure that no one will get into trouble through following my directions. If you do, and it's not just your own fault, I apologise.

1. Bowscale Fell and Bannerdale Crags

Best Map: OS 1:50,000 1¼″ to 1 mile (2cm to 1km) Landranger Sheet 90 (Penrith & Keswick). (Not on 1:25,000)

Distance: 4½ to 5½ miles/7.2km to 8.8km, depending on variation chosen

Highest elevation reached: 2306ft/703m

Height gained: 1580ft/482m

Overall star rating: * *

General level of exertion required: Medium

Time for the round: 3–3½ hours

Terrain: Mostly easy walking over grassy fells, though the descent from Bannerdale Crags requires care on the slaty rocks. An alternative descent is suggested.

Wide open spaces and rolling grassy fells characterise this walk, but there is no lack of contrast either for a gentle initial climb leads to an airy traverse around a fine cirque, an exhilarating descent and a return along the River Glenderamackin. Most of the walk would be fairly tedious in hill mist but this circuit is ideal for a day of fine weather when you feel like avoiding the crowds.

Almost midway between Keswick and Penrith, a secondary road goes off the A66 to Caldbeck and the attractive village of Mungrisdale is reached in a mile and a half. Just before you enter the village there is a clear view of the rocky end of Raven Crags straight ahead, well covered in gorse bushes, and this is the start of the walk. There is car parking on the roadside opposite the Mill Inn but it is more convenient to go further through the village, past the track signed to Mungrisdale Common (which is for the return) and past the little church. More parking places may usually be found when a fork in the road is reached, signposted for Hutton Roof (grid ref. 364306).

Immediately opposite this junction, a track leads to the right of a couple of houses. Follow this through a gate beside a little quarry and then turn immediately right up the end of the fell. A sketchy path slants up between the rocky outcrops and the gorse bushes and soon leads onto the broad whaleback of Bowscale Fell. This is uphill but easy walking, for a time through masses of bilberry, and as height is gained the whole walk becomes apparent. Bannerdale Crags become visible over the spur of The Tongue which largely obscured them from the valley, while Foule Crag and Sharp Edge on Blencathra are seen distantly.

Looking along the cirque of Bannerdale Crags; Bowscale Fell is on the right skyline

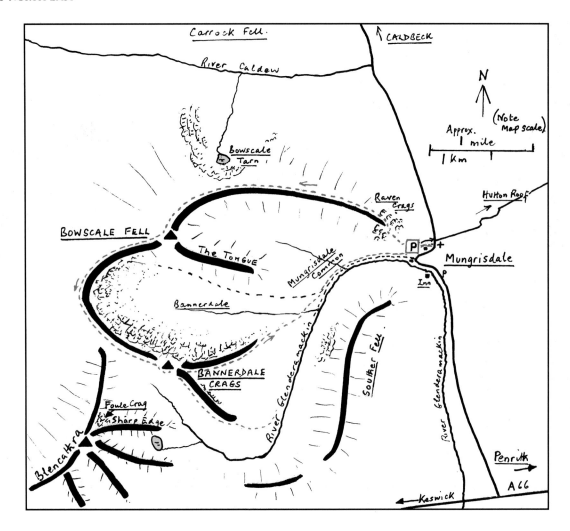

Press on towards the cairn on the skyline, but do peep over to the right just before reaching the highest point for a glimpse of Bowscale Tarn, a black pool which is visible from here although hidden from below. The access road to the mine on Carrock Fell and the buildings at the end of the road, also visible from here, are less attractive but fortunately a good distance away to the north. (The road from the mine spoils a potentially good walk over Carrock Fell, which is why it is not included in this book.)

From the cairn the way descends a little to cross a depression with a few stagnant pools in the peat, then swings round towards the cirque of Bannerdale Crags. The rocks are Skiddaw slate and well shattered but the views down Mungrisdale are worth the effort made to get here. A final pull leads up to the cairn on the highest point and an airy perch before the descent. From here a long spur projects eastwards, separating the rocky rim around which you have just walked from more, though less impressive crags further right, and this spur provides the way down. It starts on grass, rapidly leads to steeper and more shaly ground on the edge of the crags and care is needed in stepping down a couple of slate ledges. Easier terrain is soon reached and then an elegant grassy rib leads to the confluence of the Glenderamackin and the smaller beck issuing from Bannerdale. Here the path is joined leading north-eastwards along the river bank and so easily back to Mungrisdale village.

If the descent from Bannerdale Crags looks a bit too intimidating, a longer but easier way down can be found: instead of descending the spur, continue along the line of crags in a south-easterly direction until grassy slopes lead down to the Glenderamackin and the good path back to Mungrisdale.

Bannerdale Crags

11

2.   Artle Crag and Gatescarth

Best Map: OS 1:25,000 N.E. Sheet (Ullswater and Haweswater)

Distance: 4½ miles/7.2 km approx.

Highest elevation reached: 2333ft/711m

Height gained: 1600ft.488m

Overall star rating: */* * *

General level of exertion required: Fairly high

Time for the round: About 3 hours

Terrain: A mixture of paths; rolling, grassy, trackless fell; and bridleway. Reasonable visibility essential.

The head of Haweswater is for me a place charged with atmosphere; a combination of grandeur and great beauty, yet tinged with melancholy. I never saw the drowned village of Mardale Green, for the reservoir was created in the year of my birth, 1936, but – rather like Glencoe – I cannot help but be aware of its story. I have written in *On High Lakeland Fells* about the very fine circuit of Riggindale Crag, High Street

and Harter Fell, but felt that I had to find a worthwhile walk that would enable a fellwalker with less time or ambition to see this fine cirque at its best – by looking into it. The fellside between Selside and Artle Crag is really the only possibility. The walk can be done in either direction and there is perhaps more in favour of doing it the opposite way to the one I describe here because of the easier climb up the pass than up rough fellside – but then you must contain your impatience for the views, which I can never do.

I prefer to park, not in the car park at the end of the Haweswater road, but at the point where there is some space beside it, where the 'Old Corpse Road', whose lowest section to the drowned village is cut in two by the new road, leads over to Swindale from the foot of Hopgill (grid ref. 479118). It is then a steady climb up the old bridleway from the gate at the roadside up the steep curves, on the left side of Hopgill Beck, reaching first one ruined building and then another a little higher, where the bearers perhaps rested before carrying their corpse on to Swindale and then to Shap for burial. The views from up here into the great cirque of fells around the head of the reservoir are really marvellous.

Now continue a little further up the corpse road, reach some white-topped marker posts and head over

The head of Haweswater from the Old Corpse Road

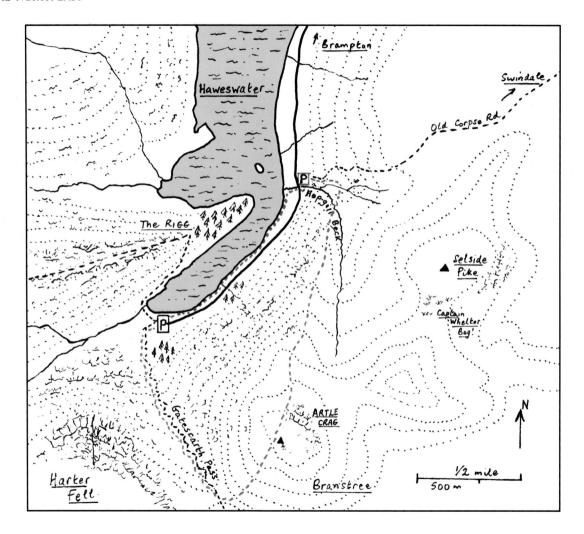

and up the moor to reach the cairn on Selside Pike, before following the broad line of the ridge south-wards over the delights of Captain Whelter Bog to reach Artlecrag Pike. Or, choosing an easier line, you may use a little sheep-track that crosses the head of Hopgill at its first feasible place above the various small cascades and then points straight at a grassy spur heading directly for what looks like the top of Artle Crag. It isn't, of course. The top, as always, is a little further back, but you'll have some good exercise climbing this grassy fellside to reach it. On a visit with my family, who remember the climb well (and won't do it again for a long time!), we had the fine sight of a small herd of deer on the distant skyline just here. A marvellous sight.

Just beyond a fine cairn near the top, you will see the seamed and craggy face of Harter Fell opposite and, five hundred feet below, the ribbon of the Gatescarth Pass track winding down to the valley again. There are no problems going down to it for it is just a grassy and stony slope. The way down the pass itself is perfectly straightforward, with a series of bends that are tight enough not to be an invitation to cut across them. They must have been good going for a packhorse.

But I was most impressed when my father-in-law, George Dracup, told me the tale of how he and five pals half-drove and half-manhandled a Morris Minor car up this very track over fifty years ago on the way to Longsleddale. He recalls staying the night in the Dun Bull in Mardale Green the night before, just a couple

of years before it vanished beneath the rising waters for ever.

Reaching the valley again you may of course walk back along the road to the car, but it's much pleasan-ter to use the lakeside path.

Looking north-west across Haweswater

15

3.   Place Fell

Best Map: OS 1:25,000 N.E. Sheet (Ullswater and
    Haweswater)

Distance: 3 miles/4.8km approx.

Highest elevation reached: 2154ft/657m

Height gained: 1650ft/503m

Overall star rating: * *

General level of exertion required: Medium/high

Time for the round: 3 hours

Terrain: Generally easy walking on good paths and
    tracks for the descent – which is the usual way
    up. The proposed way of ascent is, however, a
    bit tougher, up a natural rake line, involving
    grass, scree, boulders, not much of a path –
    and much more of an adventure.

Descending the Kirkstone Pass towards Ullswater,
Place Fell is clearly seen beyond Brothers Water,
framed by the slopes of Red Screes and those below
Raven Edge, but it is much more complex than
appears from this viewpoint and gives some excellent
fellwalking.

The most popular way up Place Fell is from Patterdale by way of the slanting track from Side Farm up
to Boardale Hause and then steeply up the shoulder of
the fell. In indifferent weather, this is probably still
the best way because the route is now so eroded and
obvious that it would be fairly hard to lose it. I did
originally intend to describe a walk over Place Fell
which goes this way, descends to near Sandwick Bay
and returns by way of Boardale, but felt that more
adventurous walkers might like to see something of
the more dramatic and secret side of Place Fell. The
ascent I recommend is a little more strenuous, much
more interesting, gives much better views over Ullswater and is a natural circular route. It is not on an
obvious ridge and not easily apparent from below,
though looking across Ullswater from Glenridding to
the west flank, several possible lines can be seen
slanting towards a shoulder of Birk Fell, which is part
of the main massif. One of these uses a stream and
does have a very sketchy path up (or, I suppose,
mostly down) it. Another is further right and is the
one to which I now refer.

There is plenty of parking at Patterdale (grid ref.
397157); then cross the valley floor either by Goldrill
Bridge or by the track near the school and beside the
George Starkey Hut to Side Farm. Pass between the
whitewashed buildings and turn left down the bridle-

*Place Fell seen from
Brothers Water*

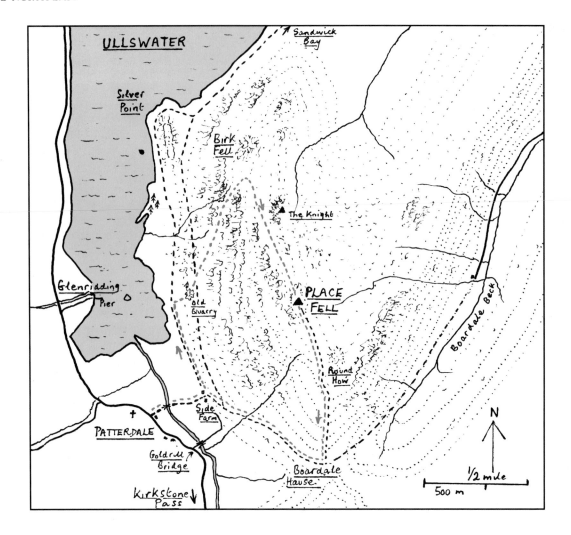

way for about a quarter of a mile alongside the wall. Just after passing a mighty and solitary oak, directly opposite the large ladder-stile (which leads over the wall into the camp-site), and before reaching a slate-built barn, turn right up the fellside through the bracken. Pass to the right of some spoil-heaps and an abandoned quarry hidden by ash trees then slant to the left across the fellside and follow the easier ground just above a rock outcrop.

Cross the well-used higher-level lakeside path and continue in the same diagonal direction below a great scree slope, above which is a belt of junipers. This natural line is interrupted occasionally by substantial scree, but don't be deflected for it gets easier as you climb steadily towards an obvious grassy shoulder, with junipers below and rockier ground above. The dark junipers can provide cover for the deer which roam the quieter parts of these fells and on the occasion when I first discovered this line I found, to my delight, that I was actually following two deer up it. The views over Ullswater are magnificent from here, high above the lake, but not obscured by the curve of the land, as is the case higher up. Continue in the same direction beyond the grassy shoulder, but now at an easier angle, towards another shoulder and then up a grassy runnel to find a cairn on a slight path. Swing sharply right now and follow a more distinct path south-eastwards, towards rock outcrops on the highest land, with another cairn ahead as your objective. A little further on, the OS triangulation point is reached, and you leave the wild country behind.

The descent is straightforward, on what is now an obvious path, south towards Round How and another cairn and then steeply down towards Boardale Hause. The final stage is the obvious track which slants to the right down the fellside back to Side Farm.

The summit of Place Fell, looking up to High Street

4. Ullswater Lakeshore

Best Map: OS 1:25,000 N.E Sheet (Ullswater and Haweswater)

Distance: 6½ miles/10.4km

Highest elevation reached: 800ft/244m

Height gained: 325ft/99m

Overall star rating: **/***

General level of exertion required: Low

Time for the round: About 4 hours, including the boat trip

Terrain: Easy going on good paths, occasionally muddy.

Ullswater has frequently been described as the most beautiful of the lakes and few will disagree. A walk along its southern shore can be delightful – but walking back the same way could be rather trying. By using the lake-steamer from Glenridding as far as Howtown, the day can be turned into a very good round trip. Obviously it is as well to check the sailing times and frequencies (usually about three times a day in summer), but once landed at Howtown the return walk takes two and a half to three hours at a gentle pace. It is an excellent family day out.

There is plenty of parking by the pier at Glenridding (grid ref. 390169); then book the single journey to Howtown, the first stop. The sail will give you a good idea of the way back on foot as you progress down the lake and the path is frequently visible along the fellside, except where it is obscured amongst the lovely woods, the juniper and the birch trees.

Leaving the jetty at Howtown, the path goes over a footbridge, along the shore, then up some steps to a higher-level terrace (with signs for Patterdale and Sandwick pointing the way all the time). The way curves under the slopes of Hallin Fell past the outcrop of Geordie's Crag and enters Hallinhag Wood where any youngsters in the party can enjoy a scramble on the rock of Kailpot Crag just inside the wood. Beyond the wood, the path leads via gates across the open fields of Sandwick to cross the Sandwick Beck, leaves the bay by going up the metalled road for a very short way and taking the Patterdale-signed path. This now undulates alongside a wall, crosses a footbridge over Scalehow Beck flowing down from the heights of Place Fell and then contours around the promontory. It has been interesting so far, but now the views really unfold as the Helvellyn massif comes into sight. The softer outlines of the fells at the northern end of the

Ullswater: the day's last ferry returns past Silver Point

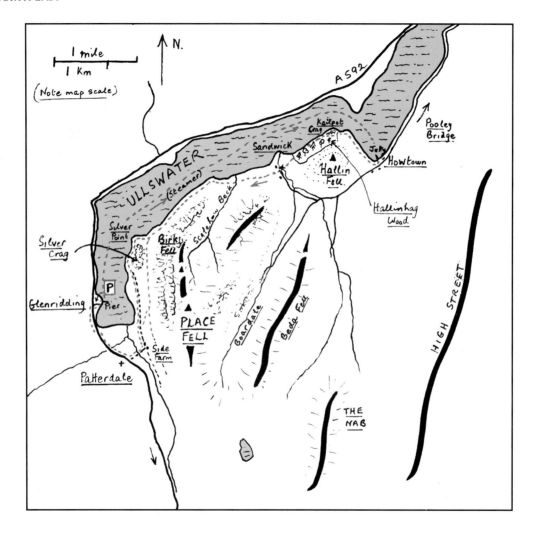

lake are left behind as the much more dramatic peaks appear ahead and a steady climb now leading to slightly higher ground allows the first of several fine prospects, made more so by the birch woods on the lower slopes of Birk Fell and the dark juniper on the higher ones.

The juniper woods on these slopes are very extensive and must certainly be the most abundant in Lakeland. When a thousand-foot-thick glacier was grinding down this valley ten thousand years ago it must have been 'real brass-monkey weather' and it isn't difficult to appreciate that only the toughest and hardiest little trees stood any chance of growth and regeneration in the hostile climate as the ice slowly retreated. But they obviously took a good hold here and have clung on ever since to this steep and craggy slope.

A little further ahead and the lake makes a sharp turn south at Silver Point where the juniper-covered and rocky hump of Silver Crag juts into the water. On reaching this, you may continue by the lakeshore past the Devil's Chimney (which is simply a tree-choked cleft – not much of a devil here) or take the more direct line which climbs to a higher level and stays up there. I prefer the higher path, for you can then more easily climb the little extra distance to the top of Silver Crag for a good view back along your walk and, if you descend the slopes a little through the tough juniper, for a most beautiful view to the head of Ullswater: the sort of view which really justifies its reputation.

It you stay on the higher path you should leave it a little way beyond the clump of trees round an old quarry to reach the main bridleway going to Side Farm – which the lower reaches anyway – then turn right across the valley bottom to Patterdale. A little tarmac-bashing is inevitable now, but after a short while, there is a path on the left of the road which is much pleasanter and leads quickly back to the field near the pier and a lakeside path to the car park.

The last stretch of the walk beside Ullswater

23

5. Sheffield Pike

Best Map: OS 1:25,000 N.E. Sheet (Ullswater and Haweswater)

Distance: 3½ or 4 miles/5.6 or 6.4km

Highest elevation reached: 2215ft/675m

Height gained: 1700ft/518m

Overall star rating: *

General level of exertion required: Medium/High

Time for the round: 2–2½ hours

Terrain: Good path for the ascent; rough and steep fellwalking on the proposed descent, so that in the event of poor weather or bad visibility it will probably be best to return by the route of ascent.

Sheffield Pike is a fine viewpoint, particularly of the Helvellyn Group and of the length of Ullswater and is itself probably best seen from the southern shore of the lake where it rises steeply above Glenridding. This walk uses the Ullswater side of the Sticks Pass for the ascent, but a steeper and more exciting way down from the tops to give a good round.

Glencoynedale is about a mile north of Glenridding and there is car parking in several places on the landward side of the main road, particularly at Glencoyne Bridge (grid ref. 387188) and also at the main road end of the track leading to the little hamlet (signed by a finger-post) of Seldom Seen. Thereafter, all the tracks or paths going west, whether skirting Glencoyne Wood or past the farmstead, lead to the well-hidden hamlet at Seldom Seen and so on to Sticks Pass. The way climbs steadily, initially alongside a wall, though with diversions around fallen storm-blown trees which block the path in places. After about 500ft of height has been gained, the path leads onto open fellside and continues upwards, towards the broad and peaty hause at the left-hand side of the head of the dale. As this is gained (the main path continuing towards Sticks Pass) a slighter path leads off left and then curves back eastwards along the broad ridge of Sheffield Pike itself. It is now only a short distance to the beacon, a pile of rocks on the summit amongst which will be found a curious stone with the characters H M E R 1830 chiselled into it, presumably the initials of an early visitor to the Pike. A little lower down is a windbreak shelter from which, in more comfort, the play of light and shade on the surrounding hills may be enjoyed.

Sheffield Pike seen across Ullswater

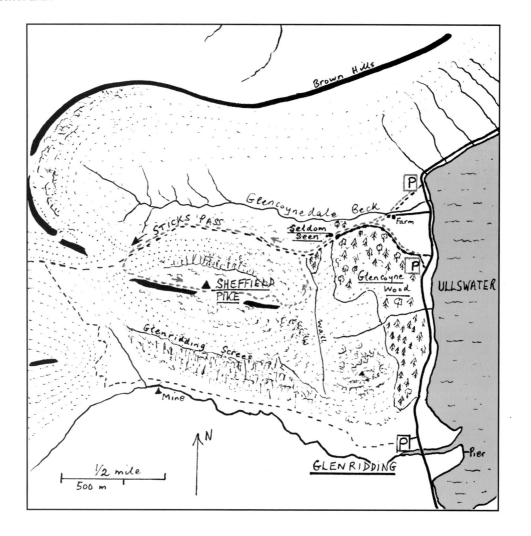

View from Sheffield Pike over Birkhouse Moor to Fairfield on the skyline

To descend, if you have come up in your wellies or your trendy canvas footwear, you had better reverse the ascent route in its entirety. If you are properly shod walk west, towards the bulk of Place Fell seen across Ullswater, following the line pointed out by about four cairns. Thereafter, there are only sketchy sheep tracks, or no tracks, to help you along, but heathery fell leads down a very broad and open gully towards Ullswater, aiming for a bare rocky top with conifers clothing its flank and a wall that runs right across and over the fell. Turn down left beside the wall outside the plantation and the Sticks Pass footpath is soon rejoined. It is now only a short descent back to the starting-point.

6. Satura Crag and Angletarn Pikes

Best Map: OS 1:25,000 N.E. Sheet (Ullswater and Haweswater)

Distance: 6 miles/9.6km

Highest elevation reached: 1900ft/579m

Height gained: 1400ft/427m

Overall star rating: * *

General level of exertion required: Medium/high

Time for the round: 3½ hours

Terrain: Good paths over most of the distance, though they aren't quite so obvious on the proposed approach to Satura Crag. This is a good walk even in mediocre weather, so long as you can see the way up.

Angle Tarn itelf is an attractive sheet of water high on the fellside at the foot of the two pikes, which stand out clearly as rocky high-points, well seen from various places on the north side of the Kirkstone Pass. This walk traverses them from that direction by way of Satura Crag.

Perhaps twenty-five years ago, some walking friends showed me a way on to the open tops above Hartsop which made use of a walled lane and a natural rake running above the line of the official right-of-way path up Hayeswater Gill. I used it a number of times, as did others, and occasionally I saw walkers descending from the tops – perhaps having lost their bearings – via this route. I believed that it constituted a permissive path but it appears I was wrong, and it doesn't, so I cannot suggest you go that way.

So, to get going, take the well-signed track leading south-east from the car park at grid ref. 410130 on the far side of Hartsop village. You will pass the sheep-pens and quickly reach a footbridge over the waters of Hayeswater Gill. A stony track now climbs more steeply up the south side of the beck and, just before reaching the weir at the mouth of Hayeswater, it crosses to the other (north) side again.

This is the beginning of a 500ft/152m climb up an often boggy slope to the east, heading for the eminence of The Knott ahead. The path then swings sharply left (north) to intersect with the path descending from its shoulder. Turn north-west now, thankfully slightly downhill, and the route undulates across the peaty flank of Rest Dodd to where it merges into a broad ridge. A wall is crossed at a gap, the path rises slightly and, just beyond a peaty hause, the rocks of Satura Crag overlook a splendid view down Bannerdale to the north.

View from Satura Crag to High Street, Hayeswater and Gray Crag

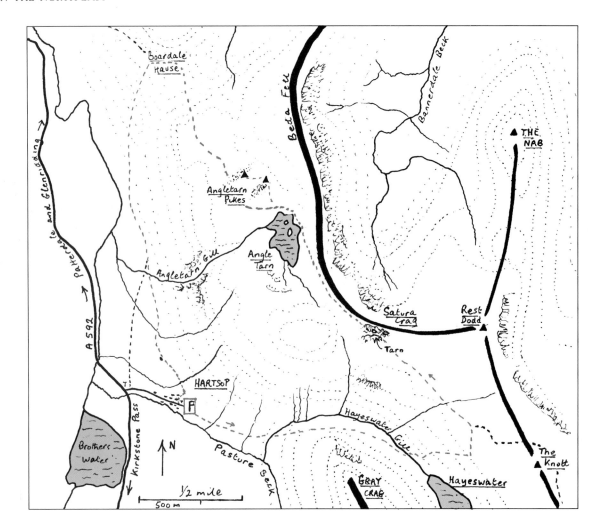

On the Hartsop side, there isn't such a distinctive crag but a search will reveal a tiny L-shaped tarn trapped amongst the rocks. This is a spot which provides a dramatic perch for the superb views to High Street, Hayeswater and Gray Crag in particular. It is a great place for a pause.

Walking north-westwards now soon brings Angle Tarn into view. It is delightfully situated, with several little islands and a craggy shore on its far side. The path skirts the tarn but here is a great chance to scramble to the summits above it, for these are the Angletarn Pikes themselves. The views are good, but it's the scrambling up there that makes them better still, and it is easy to spend time here before you return to the path.

This is well worn now (in fact, there is both a lower and a higher path but they join further on so it doesn't matter which you take) and leads easily to the meeting of ways on Boardale Hause. You won't find the 'Chapel in the Hause' which is marked on the Ordnance Survey map, though you may find a few scattered and no doubt consecrated stones.

Here swing to the left beside the beck, then cross it and follow the obvious path down a track which is alternately stony and grassy, taking a slanting diagonal line beside the buried (but detectable) water conduit towards Brothers Water.

At the foot of Angletarn Gill, rather than taking the footbridge leading to the lower-level lane returning to Hartsop, cross the footbridge but then go along the wall for thirty paces until a stone stile leads across

it to a much more interesting footpath. This leads past the beautifully situated house called 'Grey Rigg' and then goes directly to the upper part of Hartsop village and the car park.

Angle Tarn from near one of its Pikes, looking south

31

7.   Gowbarrow Fell

Best Map: OS 1:25,000 N.E. Sheet (Ullswater and
Haweswater)

Distance: 3½ miles/5.6km approx.

Highest elevation reached: 1578ft/481m

Height gained: 1100ft/335m

Overall star rating: * * / * * *

General level of exertion required: Fairly low

Time for the round: 2–3 hours

Terrain: Mostly on good paths over grassy fellside
but with the odd rougher and boggier patch.
There should be few problems in less than
perfect weather.

To wander over Gowbarrow Fell, with its wonderful views over Ullswater, then to return via the spectacular cascade of Aira Force (avoiding nearly all the 'tourist-zone' down near the lakeside) is a delightful experience and this walk describes such a possibility.

The A5091 links the A66 Penrith–Keswick road with that along the north shore of Ullswater (the A592), passing through the village of Dockray. This road climbs towards Dockray from the lakeside and just before reaching the village, there is a quarry on the left and a large lay-by on the right-hand side with the sign 'National Trust Gowbarrow', which is a good place to park (grid ref. 396212). The sign also supposedly restricts your length of stay here – a bit of bureaucracy that is rightly ignored by all who don't intend to be rushed over their enjoyment of such a fine walk as this. Perhaps it's intended to restrict you from having a picnic by the river bank? A footpath leads down the fields from here to Aira Beck and this is crossed by means of a 'strid' over the limestone blocks through which the water rushes at its narrowest point. You can quite literally stand with one foot on one side and one on the other here but if your nerves won't stand this, you can go downstream for a couple of hundred paces to find a footbridge and then go back up the other bank. (Don't waste your time going upstream before crossing because the way is barred). If you park in Dockray itself after the road has crossed the beck, there is a path along the other bank. Personally I prefer the little excitement of the strid.

Now go upstream on the east bank for a hundred paces and then follow various paths and sheep tracks slanting uphill and leftwards to the north-east, wandering up through the bracken, to reach the trig point

*Walkers on Green Hill;
looking across Ullswater
to Hallin Fell and the
Martindale Fells*

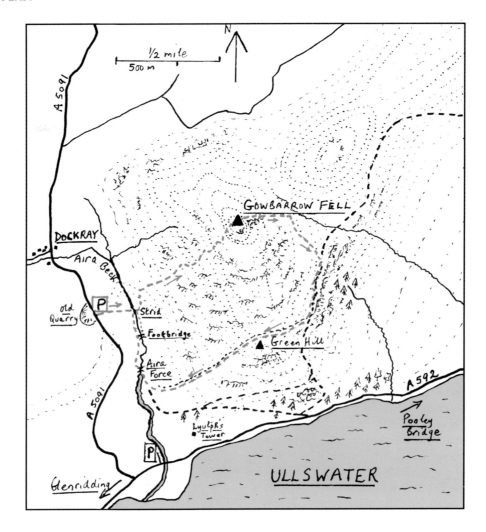

on the summit. There are no worthwhile views from here, for a brackeny moor blocks the prospect over Ullswater, but descend a little spur from the summit towards a stile in a corner where two walls meet and this leads to a little beck tinkling towards Ullswater. Swing sharply right before meeting the stream and cross rougher ground for a little way before descending gently to intersect with a good path which now contours the side of the fell above Ullswater. This is a delightful path, virtually level for much of the way, skirting just above little crags and woods and heading generally towards the lake.

When a choice of ways arrives, take the right fork, which quickly leads up to the superb viewpoint of Green Hill, a little eminence on the fellside which gives lovely views along the lake and particularly towards its head. We stood here once when the sky turned almost black overhead and it looked as if a mighty downpour was about to start. But then a shaft of sunlight struck down through the clouds and illuminated, spotlit, an area of Patterdale. Slowly it travelled up the fellside towards the higher peaks and then disappeared. Then within five minutes the clouds rolled back and the risk of a cloudburst passed.

From here a good path now slants gently downhill across the fell towards Aira Beck, passing above the battlements and turrets of Lyulph's Tower, and joining the main path to Aira Force just before reaching the footbridge which spans the cascade at its top. It's almost always worth making the short descent to the viewpoint below the falls because they are most

Aira Force

spectacular seen from there, then circling up the other side (on a good path) back to the bridge. Now leave the tourists rushing back to their coaches and teas and wander back upstream on a good path, but on the left-hand side of the Aira Beck, to reach another but much shorter cascade. Just above it is the strid again and the footpath back over the fields to the car.

8. Hallin Fell

Best Map: OS 1:25,000 N.E. Sheet (Ullswater and Haweswater)

Distance: 2 miles/3.2km approx. (plus steamer journey)

Highest elevation reached: 1271ft/387m

Height gained: 770ft/235m

Overall star rating: * *

General level of exertion required: Medium

Time for the round: 4 hours, including the boat trip.

Terrain: Generally easy going on good paths or grassy slopes. The low altitude of the fell means that it is often well below the prevailing cloud ceiling.

Hallin Fell projects boldly into Ullswater on its south-eastern shore. It's only a little tiddler, but it's quite isolated from the surrounding fells, a splendid viewpoint and the more noticeable for having a tall stone obelisk, visible for miles, on its summit. The ascent can be made in a twenty-minute burst of energy, or it can be treated as a really enjoyable walk in its own right, very suitable for a family walk (however you define it), a short day, or even a long one if you stop often enough. I prefer wild country to the other sort and so this walk deliberately chooses a natural line to the top.

For most people coming from the other side of Ullswater, reaching Howtown from Patterdale via Pooley Bridge is a time-consuming hassle, unless you take the lake steamer starting from the pier at Glenridding. There is ample parking there (grid ref. 390169), the boat sails regularly, gives a scenic trip along the best part of Ullswater and makes its first stop at Howtown. Make sure you check the return times so there is ample opportunity to climb Hallin Fell and return the same way. (I may add that on a recent visit, by road, there had been so much rain that Ullswater was slopping over the tarmac and a boat would have been needed to reach the dry land even from the Howtown jetty, but these were exceptional circumstances.)

From the jetty at Howtown, follow the path over a footbridge and along the lake shore through a couple of wicket-gates, following signs for Patterdale and Sandwick all the time, up some steps and turn right onto a terrace well above the shoreline, alongside a wall. The path runs parallel to the lakeside, turns the

Hallin Fell seen across Ullswater

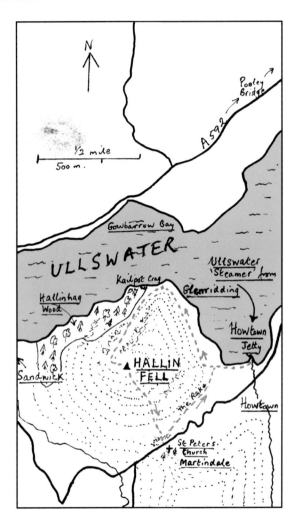

corner and approaches Kailpot Crag just inside Hallinhag Wood. Immediately before entering the wood, an infrequently used path goes left, climbing steeply through the bracken and between two rock outcrops, one a little higher than the other. Above the higher rocks, the bracken is much less dense, the angle eases and a slanting, natural grassy rake leads upwards and across a fellside, just below the line of the ridge which is itself a little higher up. There is a path of sorts, used by sheep and a few other wanderers like yourself: nothing much, but enough.

Nearing a shoulder of the fell, the rake comes to an end and you must scramble very easily upwards to the fine obelisk on the summit. This is about twelve feet high and six feet broad at its base, built mostly of granite (or something like that – I'm no geologist) but with two blocks of a softer stone inset high up, one above the other, on the northern side. On the upper stone (amongst other carvings, mostly the scratchings of hooligans, are chiselled the initials IW. SP 19. On the lower one there is a large letter B and, more faintly, the date 1864. Perhaps to commemorate the builder? Whoever he was, he certainly built a solid monument on a fine viewpoint. Have a look at the Martindale fells from here: some splendid walking country.

The descent is easier and very straightforward. Go down the grassy slopes on any of several paths which are all close together, heading for the nearest building in sight, which is St Peter's Church, Martindale. This is situated on a hause, with a clump of sheltering

Looking north from Place Fell, with Hallin Fell in the middle distance

trees, where the road climbs in hairpin-bends round the back of Hallin Fell into Martindale. Cars are often parked here, opposite the church, while their owners take the soft option of climbing the fell with this little height advantage. Don't walk down the road, for a grass track called The Rake leads directly from the hause at a much more gentle angle back towards the Howtown jetty.

39

9.   Gill Crag Ridge and Dovedale

Best Map: OS 1:25,000 N.E. Sheet (Ullswater and Haweswater)

Distance: 4 miles/6.4km approx.

Highest elevation reached: 1870ft/570m

Height gained: 1350ft/411m

Overall star rating: *

General level of exertion required: Medium

Time for round: 2½–3 hours

Terrain: A sketchy path to the ridge, a good one on it, a rougher descent, but then a good path down Dovedale. Because this is essentially a ridge walk, it gives few problems even in mist.

This walk is very simple in concept: climb up to and walk the ridge overlooking both Deepdale and Dovedale, with splendid views of the heads of both, then descend the beautiful Dovedale to return. It gives the best of the views without having to do either of the greater cirques of Dovedale or Deepdale.

There is a good car park at the northern end of Brothers Water (grid ref. 403134) just where the A592 crosses the Goldrill Beck and there is a useful and interesting National Park signboard about the particular problems of farming in Dovedale just beside the track which leads southwards along the west side of Brothers Water. Don't rush off along the track though, because immediately beyond the signboard a path, not always obvious, particularly in summer when the trees are in leaf, climbs steeply into Low Wood to the right of the main track. In a few yards, there is a stile and then another with a thoughtful little gate at its foot which can be lifted to let an animal through. I personally appreciate this because then I don't have to lift the muddy little bodies of my two Schnauzers. The path, rather sketchy in places, now climbs steadily towards the ridge above. As it gets above the tree line, you see a fine prospect of Brothers Water and many of the High Street fells, with the attractive village of Hartsop nestling below.

The path begins to peter out but then the line of an old collapsed wall is reached and this can be followed up the fellside to reach a cairn. Ahead is a very solid wall, running down the length of the main ridge. Don't attempt to cross this here; stay to the left of the wall on the sketchy path until you reach a stile, then cross over to the main line of the ridge. You will have fine views across Dovedale up to this point. The ridge is now broad and open until the rockier high ground

Looking up Dovedale from Brothers Water

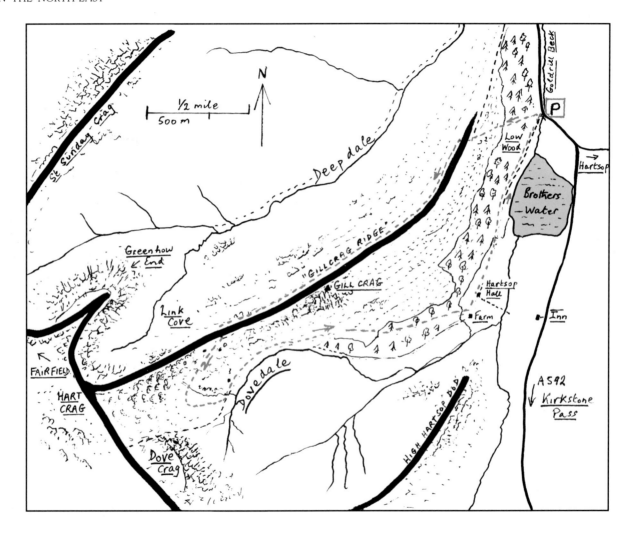

of Gill Crag is reached, and then there are increasingly good views of the magnificent wild head of Deepdale with Link Cove and Greenhow End on the right side and the impressive cliffs of Dove Crag – scene of many great rock-climbing epics – on the left. Beyond Gill Crag the ridge is broader again and, as you progress, the ground becomes more like a Derbyshire moor, with peat-hags and rocky outcrops and the path winding amongst them, before it begins a slow climb towards the heights of Hart Crag ahead.

Now leave the beaten track and veer to the left, slanting across the fell towards Dove Crag, choosing your own line but not losing height and, though you may be tempted, not descending the course of the beck which goes down rather too abruptly for comfort. Cross the beck to get nearer to Dove Crag and you will intersect with a path which will be found going down a normally dry and fairly shallow gully. This now leads fairly steeply downhill past a ruined building and becomes steadily better as it reaches more level ground.

The last stage of this walk down Dovedale is really a delightful one, downhill all the way to the valley floor, on a path which goes just above the beck and then wanders through ancient woods, with glimpses all the time of the greener pastures below and the sound of the tumbling waters always in your ears. Beyond the farm buildings, the way leads round to the back of Hartsop Hall and joins a level farm track which enables you to wander along the side of the beautiful Brothers Water and back to the car park.

The head of Deepdale from the Gill Crag ridge above Brothers Water

43

10. Gray Crag

Best Map: OS 1:25,000 N.E. Sheet (Ullswater and Haweswater)

Distance: 5 miles/8km

Highest elevation reached: 2331ft/710m

Height gained: 1850ft/564m

Overall star rating: *

General level of exertion required: Medium

Time for the round: 3 hours

Terrain: Good paths and easy walking except for the stony section above Threshthwaite Cove which can be loose, slippery and not very enjoyable in bad weather. The final descent is steep but it is generally a straightforward outing.

Gray Crag is rather like a neglected central prong in a trident, ignored in favour of its eastern neighbour, High Street, but it is a shapely fell in its own right and usually peaceful when the crowds are tramping the old Roman roadway. On three occasions, I have seen a small herd of deer move quickly away up the slopes of Gray Crag as I drew close, but I have never seen them on High Street. I hear so often the cry that the Lake District is crowded, but there are lots of places to go that aren't – when you know where they are. This is one of them.

The start is at the very attractive village of Hartsop, just beyond Brothers Water on the north side of the Kirkstone Pass, and the car park is at grid ref. 410130 on the far side of the village. As you enter, the steep end of Gray Crag is very evident straight ahead. We are, however, going to steal up on it from behind and use that blunt nose as the way down. So, going through the car park gate, turn right immediately and follow the 'Pasture Beck' sign over the stream and then left up its right bank (true left, in the direction of flow) through sheep pastures, to the final intake wall, gate and stile. (The main path to Hayeswater Gill is seen on the other (left) side of the valley floor).

The path now stays close to the course of the beck, with the hause, col, or pass of Threshthwaite Mouth ahead as its obvious objective, though it is probably of more recent origin than the Roman way which used Hagg Gill on the far side and climbed more rapidly to the then more defensible and less afforested ridges. It passes below steep crags on the west side (Raven Crag, Threshthwaite Mouth) which have seen some

Gray Crag from the village of Hartsop

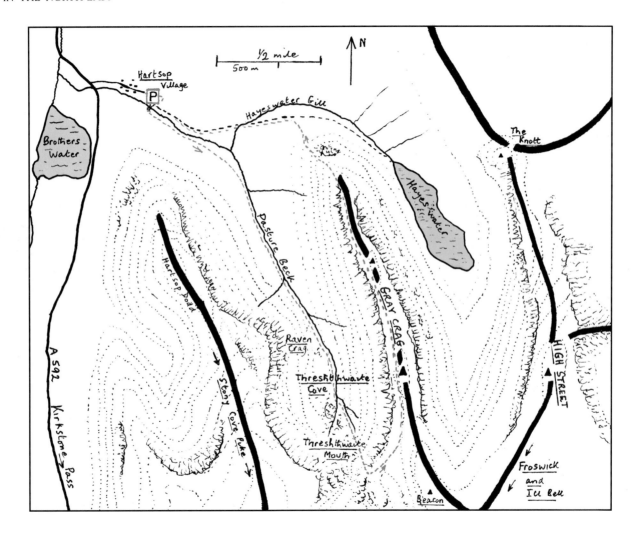

of the most recent rock-climbing developments in the area and then becomes less obvious as it wanders amongst rocks and stones on the last section.

Reaching the pass go left up scrabbly scree and rocks – the path is steep and loose here and crampons are often needed in winter – but as height is gained, veer to the left side of the tumbledown wall, cross the remains of another and head for the broad grassy ridge of Gray Crag itself. You will shortly be able to have your lunch in solitude, although if it's windy you will have to tuck yourself into a grough between peat-hags or hide in a grassy hollow, for it is exposed to the elements up here. You won't be troubled by the litter and orange peel around Threshthwaite Beacon just a little distance away and will be able to enjoy much the same views to High Street, down to Hayeswater and of course to Ullswater.

For the descent, continue northwards. The path along the summit ridge peters out as others before you have sought for the best line of descent and been undecided. I think it is best to go straight down initially, but there is an outcrop of steep rocks just a little way down the end of the fell and it's best to trend slightly to one side of the ridge to avoid them. If you go left, you can follow the line of a wall which goes part of the way down the fell and then, for no apparent reason, ends. It could hardly have been a shortage of stone. However, just beyond this is a corner of the intake-field wall, beside which is the main Hayeswater Gill track which leads back to the car park.

Looking up Pasture Beck to Threshthwaite Mouth, with Gray Crag on the left

47

INDEX